AVAILABLE LIGHT

Available Light

Poems by
Audrey Rooney

Accents Publishing • Lexington, Kentucky • 2019

Copyright © 2019 by Audrey Rooney
All rights reserved

Printed in the United States of America

Accents Publishing
Editor: Katerina Stoykova-Klemer
Cover Illustration: "Regalia" by Audrey Rooney

Library of Congress Control Number:
ISBN: 978-1-936628-52-0
First Edition

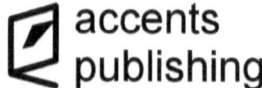 accents publishing

Accents Publishing is an independent press for brilliant voices. For a catalog of current and upcoming titles, please visit us on the Web at

www.accents-publishing.com

CONTENTS

At Snug Hollow Farm / 3
Plein Air / 4
Interlace / 5
Synchrony / 6
Midden / 7
White Noise / 8
Private Property / 9
Embouchure / 10
Ear Ring / 11
Civil Twilight Kenwick / 12
Trash Tuesday / 13
Essential Oil / 14
Narcissus / 15
Mantis / 16
Osage Boundary / 17
Sacrifice / 18
Interment / 19
Afterimage / 20
Two Domestic Devotions / 21
Recycling / 22
Of Skeps and Skeptics / 23
Skywalker / 24
Firepoem / 25
Chasing *Le Mot Juste* / 26
Remorse / 27
Self Study / 28
Aura / 29
Chiaroscuro / 30
Vintage / 31
Opposable Thumb / 32
Catch and Release / 33
Bon Appétit / 34
Coup de Grâce / 35
Darcy's Ashes Wouldn't Fill a Demitasse / 36
Reception / 37

First Death / 38
Quickening / 39
Overture / 40
Ohio Approach / 41
SOS / 42
Scavenger Hunt / 43

About the Author / 45

Acknowledgments / 47

To my children
Melinda and Alec

AT SNUG HOLLOW FARM
for Barbara, Rhonda, Olivia, Kerry & All

I must learn new languages here
how to speak in Gold or Bark or Moss
and in the many tongues of Lichen spangled
on a triple stemmed maple   decline new
nouns, conjugate the verb 'to stark'
as in naked trees raking a pine-furred hillside
bones pale as ivory hoarding available light
To interpret calls in warm November dark
   learn Owl

I'll grow fluent in Chill so you can feel
what I feel when grayed shawls of dusk
close in   settle on my skin
    share my fire

PLEIN AIR

      Osage
       orange
        tree stump
      struck by lightning
     its core an embryo
    curled within
  a spiral
   crevice
  where recent
    saw-marks
      slanted
       gouge suggest
   a sundial faded rings
   girdle the sapling's birth
   day measure girth seasons
    flowering fruiting until
     electric event
    end of story

Now let your watercolor say all this

INTERLACE

Awake Before Ireland

In high blue-eyed sky harvest moon weaves
her gilded basketry through old cherry-tree boughs
pock-marked satin trunk snags loops of light tossed
down to rippling fish pond where they join in
wayward circles and tatter in the breeze

Awake Leaving Ireland

From roundabout to roundabout sulphur
lamps warm a foggy dawn on Shannon airport
road soundless rain fans coach window in bright
diagonals invites Venn circles to rise like halos
geometries geographies your soft incendiary kiss

SYNCHRONY

Time already hours short of a lunar month to turn
my amber hourglass honey jar nearly empty
snugly capped upside down for the night
sweetness pooling in the lid till before
morning light when I dipstick what
is left into hot tea to begin anew
my fragile truce with
time

MIDDEN

Rummaging deep in the freezer yesterday turning
over bags of blueberries blintzes pea soup two

pewter skinned brook trout near the bottom numb
fingers closed on a heel of brown bread a surprise

My cupped hands held what's left of what your earthy
golden hands mixed and let rise pummeled caressed

and baked last summer then brought to me   to us

Today the thawed bread smells oven fresh as it falls
in crusty slices under my mother-in-law's rough blade

of carbon steel I break the end chunk in pieces taste again
the rich plainness of you a quarter-curve of earth away
and fill my mouth with absence two for breakfast ever?

Who says half a loaf is better than none?

WHITE NOISE

Terra firma too much with me
  glaring moon no lullaby
     draw shades
    turn covers down
  smooth pillows
     set phone app
    go deep
  to caroling whales

aeons long unknown songs
    in canyons fathoms
       down
   seabed to curling
 billows
     rhapsodies
   wooing
  small talk
    goodbyes

hours glide toward morning
    sink surface
     sink again
      dozing
     dreaming I hear
  oboe d'amore
    say yes
  to bass trombone

PRIVATE PROPERTY

Seen in the right light morning in Siena invites
imaginings larger and longer than both our lives
as two espresso cups empty too soon

Across the street blue iron filigree railings
embrace a balcony's pink walls red geraniums
and a sign we recite to soften our consonants

        Proprietà Privata

Sing like you say *gelato* you tell me and we laugh

EMBOUCHURE

Hey
I just dialed your Master Key
pitch pipe around to B
thirty years after dropping
it on the floor in Siena
You agreed I should replace it so
in Florence I bought you another

In the morning before I sing
Dvorak's Psalm 23
at a midsummer graveside
I'll rest my lips on
the mouthpiece   softly breathe
that kiss we missed back then

EAR RING

    for Raleigh Jones, MD

                         Praise
                all things spiral
             sunflower whorls
           bindweed twining
        strangling the fiddleheads
      pinecones
    pineapple rind possum
  dung coiled shining
in the grass
 ammonite fossils under our
   feet in spoil banks
    along the C & D
     canal   DNA
       Vatican's double
         helix staircase
          golden means
            twin f holes on a violin
             deep in my ears
               twin cochlea snails
                 ornaments of hearing
                   truth receivers falsehood
                 deceivers   penny
              whistles sleigh bells
            constant concert A
        in late years
          Niagara pulse
       drowns them all

CIVIL TWILIGHT KENWICK

Halfway to equinox   not yet dawn
scrim veils the garden in a spell
of time known as civil twilight
last most luminous of three
twilights that herald the sun
feel garden holding its breath
a colossal stillness on the turning
earth as her brightening curve meets
the sun waiting in the holiness of not yet

TRASH TUESDAY

Dung beetles of the dawn   two grey
one azure big as boxcars snort chirp
paw street beneath my bedroom window

First grey sprouts giant tongs   reaches
shrieking skyward   dives to bin of lawn
waste on the curb leggy mint   yarrow

dogwood boughs grass clippings Silage
scents autumn breeze sinks into monster
salad in the tank   Second grey hoists

household stench   shakes rotten leftovers
Halloween pretzels gone to dust cat poop
litter will spice a block party potluck stew

Choosy big blue bangs hisses stomachs
only recyclables   plastic clamshells juice
bottles morning paper pizza boxes phone

books catalogs most of the mail but NO
cloth styrofoam peanuts wire coat hangers
plastic bags lightbulbs especially curly ones

Like cleansing Fates ravening trash trucks
bring order to our chaos   each demanding
specific cargo we spend our lives sorting

ESSENTIAL OIL

Unscrew blue vial
draw deep breath, smell smoke
A pub's turf fire in county Clare?
Nothing nearly so cozy comforting
instead disturbing earthy potent honest
won't promise you a rose garden
more like burnt manure
Just the facts ma'am

Is this why I crave
a whiff before bed on waking?
Because vetiver clears my head
keeps me real? So I can be damn
sure that whatever I meet
asleep or on the street
has to be gentler simpler
sweeter than this?

NARCISSUS

Five mourning doves perch on a power line
two pairs plus a loner   still as glazed
museum pieces an audience eyeing me
damp bewildered down below softly
    cursing the sprinkler.

Idle in the garage all winter now its dumb
insolence sits in my lap - four yellow arms
inert to my flimsy grasp of male female
left right - manage a feeble trickle
    into my shoes.

Whose point of view do I assume here
mine — after all I am holding the hose —
or the sprinkler's? More to the point must
I relearn this every spring? Apparently yes.
Give in to the sprinkler get the hell
    out of my own way.

MANTIS

Strung up in the crown vetch
a corpse hanged in effigy
spun sugar sprite

oval head flattened
dark feelers fine
as fetal hairs

fringed pincers at prayer
hinged limbs akimbo
child's drawing of Daddy

Stuck in spider silk
my fingers feel
not death   rather

escape to life
last night's web holding fast
goblin's infant self

shrugging off skin
an adolescent born
soon departing

OSAGE BOUNDARY

                three osage
           oranges left in lapping
           tide stud the river shore
           bright knobby rinds cast
             three purple smudges
              on shining sand

    brought down
in the night by weight
and wind they rest in a still
life oblivious to their fellows
and such puzzles as where
   does water end and
      land begin

              once in demand as
             poor man's barbed wire
          a phalanx thick with savage
         thorns hedged every farmstead
       here no need no harvests now only
      scattered baubles small boys take
        for their mothers to decorate
           kitchen windowsills

SACRIFICE

Of three d'Anjou pears on the butcher block
this one seemed to glow with a unique sense of self
I was almost sorry to see it ripen but when we could wait
no longer I set it in the window   found paper and pastels
and worked big   quartered for lunch tasted of Eden

INTERMENT

Stretched on pavement mid-leap   young squirrel   glazed left eye gazing
nowhere on its flank fly-egg flecks   no mark no wound   tail at half-mast
in my hands rigid   cooler than August afternoon   in my ears urgent

humming as sparkly flies come circling round   must bury it   and soon
soil packed hard   crusted mulch   black seed hulls slow jabbing spade
after ten years still poor at graveyard duty rest a moment muse on brief

life brought low from high wire somersaults   tipping birdbaths   routing
wrens   standoffs over stale baguettes   dig some more   reach soft earth
lay him down   cover his tinseled plume   aware I've changed a pronoun

AFTERIMAGE

Off the Atlantic coast of Mayo
Irish optics play as the sea so the sky
clouds and swells scumble dark to bright
our red boots glow ponchos match
the yellow gabled shrine where coiled line
and red ring-buoy hang close by a sign

A STOLEN RING-BUOY - A STOLEN LIFE

Who would steal a ring-buoy ?

We voyeurs — call us tourists —have crossed
the Michael Davitt bridge to Achill island
mustering now near Keel village where
potato farmers lived until they starved

Huddled on a cliff curled over pulsing surf
we stare at foam dandling a kelp-strewn strand
Spotting a sailor's grave we pretend to read words
to his mother carved in Finnish we watch
a godlike surfer take a wave

Turning then to whitewashed ruins sunk in wet
grass pausing to adore twin lambs asleep in a cleft
of shadow we see for the first time in our lives
the color green: muddied drab palest winter-kill
emerald neon super-saturated shamrocks trick
our retinas set rods and cones spinning

Squinting skyward I see a mirage all crimson
think stolen lives ask did dying eyes see
last horizons of home in imperial red ?

TWO DOMESTIC DEVOTIONS

Grace before lunch after a crummy start to the day

Thank you
   brown eggs
under cool
running water
for slipping
so graciously out
of your shells
   and you
avocado remnant
for remaining
green   yielding to me
your small shining
pit   shaped like
a robin's egg

RECYCLING

January first taking measure
of last year's moons waxing
full   waning new   cutting
folding dimensions short
and long to line a kitchen drawer
so that in the twelve months
to come under skewers spatulas
pastry brushes pasta tongs
and slotted spoons I'll glimpse
a perfect fit   buried treasure
motion stilled panoply of light
grace all foretold   specific
as it should be

OF SKEPS AND SKEPTICS

Drinking honey-laced tea checking Snopes to find out if Einstein really said — or wrote — "if the bee disappeared off the surface of the earth, then man would have only four years of life left."

Rather than FALSE or TRUE Snopes rules the claim UNDETERMINED Why? Because no records of his saying so — or writing so — exist. A letdown but what an excellent thought to ponder.

Grateful for skeptics busy combing data for benefit of truth, we are reminded that we are still at liberty to behave as if it were so.

SKYWALKER

        Quaker
    Luke Howard named
the clouds and winds for us
     shut out from University
Law the Church shy London lad
took scientific circles by storm
    taking holy orders
        from the sky

FIREPOEM

Gather dry leaves teased bark thready
lightweight in the hand   when compressed

omnipotent find kindling crack deadwood
branchlets break brittle twigs   split rough

boughs for longer burning   all will matter
choose to seek heat   or wait for it   pass sun

through pocket lens   point a ruby laser
foment friction   stroke stick on stick

light caresses first   pressing harder feel
heat stir inertia   bring mouth close softly

blow seize moment as kindling ignites
twigs tented crosswise like a wigwam

purpose essential   risk more so
this once   let a little hell break loose

CHASING LE MOT JUSTE

Spot it at last or so you think
    creep up on it to lure
        surprise it
        net in hand
      Nabokov in mind
    turn net trap
      then release
        into
          killing
              jar

REMORSE

She should have arisen
this morning at three

wrapped up in fleece
brewed chamomile tea

switched on the light
entertained similes

snapping like popcorn
in dream-strewn debris

this linking with that
allusions set free

start day with the poem
on intimacy

but body and spirit
refused to agree

and on waking at six
all absentee

SELF STUDY

Our bodies mobile continents of flesh and blood held
on short or long-term lease come tricked out with nets
of labyrinths where energy sound light memory breath
and all sensations travel — paprika on the tongue? has
rain begun? — ideally unimpeded Young in prime time
or abundant autumn years we embrace the givenness of
our animated selves barely aware of hidden avenues wide
open for business pleasure   Long-term lessors learn

better Channels once accommodating become less so
dams logjams slow data flow Bronchioles arterial
walls narrow bones meet marrow crush nerves cloud
brain mute joy send pain unwanted agendas swell
our brains in silent treatment rooms we wait killing
time reading charts of labyrinths arrayed like rainbows

AURA
for Dr Oliver Sacks

At first invisible
there but not there
infinitesimal   g a p
something missing
  in ring
of flames heating
black and white
checkered teakettle

Certainty of fireworks
to come   soon   twinkling
wreath quivering

dilate shrink   dilate
unwind   up
down left right and
wherever I look
the bullseye
is blank

black strong coffee
lights out   no
headache anymore
now
that I'm old

CHIAROSCURO

Sun mops up rain drops
   mourning doves toll passing bell
for five drowned starlings

Deep in waiting bed
   red emperor tulip bulb
slips into darkness

Snail's pace traffic jam
   parts waves in sunflower sea
eclipses don't wait

Bright airfoils grounded
   marmalade cat's nightwork
quick! paper and paints

Late Bruch concerto
   shadows dance on copper tray
French kiss of coffee

VINTAGE

                  Concord
           grapes washed wet
       on wet a century ago hang
     from a twig curved slightly left
    suggesting a letter C perhaps for
    Cora Reed   the young artist
  my mother's mother my grandma
each fruit life-size   at ease in its own
skin claims lights   and   hollows
   assumes myriad blues purples
   loamy darks in yeasty blushing
      harmonies of plenty
          in early girlhood profound
       deafness struck   now her aging
       granddaughter hearing none
       too well   sees Cora touching
         tasting showing how
           light caresses life
           in silence

OPPOSABLE THUMB

My right thumb mounts ever more frequent opposition to
my intent to thread a needle, open a marmalade jar, turn a key
pry a paint can lid loose, prune a quince twig, sift a cup of flour.

How many million years in the making, this huge evolutionary
reach? Lending a hand to the handy man *homo habilis* and all
of us men and women - handy or not - to follow?

Come on, thumb, remember what a game-changer this was
for the Pleistocenes? Hang on a little longer, let me pop a few
more champagne corks, write one last legible thank-you note?

CATCH AND RELEASE

Nearsighted   aching back   swaddled in aqua towel
draw bathwater   steamy thunderclouds   smell like
sesame   candle flame sputters   what about a feathery
straw colored thing   swirling in the current   alive
or cat fur fluff   can't find my glasses   grab brass snuffer
try scooping   alive it is   frantic many-legged swimmer
off to kitchen for tea strainer   return   find thing inert
on the bottom   one swipe   draped supine in the mesh

Weightless   may be dead   crush or flush   instead
bring as offering to patio table frosty night no moon
eyes dark adapt   leave curled fringe in repose till dawn
find strainer empty learn centipedes nearly blind
— that made two of us— forward fangs hold poison
bite seldom lethal   relearn rescue laced with risk

BON APPÉTIT

After spending Sunday afternoon reading book reviews about
the Bolsheviks a century ago   I'm not hungry tonight so grateful
for soup I made yesterday   a plain thin soup of celery potato
onion water very little milk   it kept wanting salt   I roasted
a game hen too   and as I daubed her with butter   trussed her
with twine one vertebra fell loose at her neck where her head
had been   a watch-charm glistening   soup simmers on
the fire   incites the air   now I am hungry and cannot eat

COUP DE GRÂCE

Squirrel squads beheaded my garden patriarch
yesterday a Mammoth Russian holding sway
all summer over upstart sunflowers an arm's
length off sown by goldfinch dynasties

Gnomon of my living sundial hairstreaks
wrens and chickadees feasted at your face
rings of bell moths rested there till dark

Now dead leaves point like semaphores
from a shepherd's crook down to the
spent seedhead haloed in bright darts
   what's left of your corona

DARCY'S ASHES WOULDN'T FILL A DEMITASSE

Feline familiar sentinel was he
liaison amid the mysteries
of a couple growing old
kept watch over a deathbed
rode wide awake silhouetted
on the rear windshield shelf from
Maryland to Kentucky drooling
then found his heart's desire at
a Hampton Inn asleep against my feet

Decades ago small skeletons
had begun to wreathe our far-flung
rural and urban homesteads hamsters
canaries   a white kitten born dead
zebra finches a hermit crab
a basset hound covered with wild flowers
now I crouch sifting mortal crumbs
of Darcy across a hand's breadth of early snow

RECEPTION

How we squandered you and I as
if we had eternity to hear each other
missing cues   antennae out of tune
sharing with all things created
nature's wastefulness
profligate as August's host
of tattered mourning cloaks
welded in bright mosaics
to SUV grilles at the Chesapeake
Bay Bridge Tunnel rest stop

But I recall the noontime
I unfastened one and brought it
purple wings slowly fanning
to you   we walked a stretch
of concrete and steel spanning
two Virginia coasts to find
some shade   where I
soaked my handkerchief
with ice melt from your soft
drink cup and we laid
the butterfly
down

FIRST DEATH

> *Child, drowned by an alligator at Disney World*
> *August 2016*
> *after Dylan Thomas*

My fail-safe psalm
fails   No shepherd there

beside still waters. Only
baby steps bliss

of wet sand   small hands
busy at scoop and pail

in tall reeds where
hinged daggers glide

lunge open wide
slam shut

'After the first death there is no other'

QUICKENING
for Jim

With another nondescript Kentucky winter done I'm keeping up our old twilight ritual poking around the garden to check for signs of life   how we knelt in drab perennial beds turning up color   knuckles of rhubarb coiled shrimp-flower ferns bloodroot rhizomes   rosy earthworms breaking first ground On one early March walkabout three of us made the rounds   our muddy hands smoothed the swell of my corduroy smock and felt our first child stir   you anatomist of the equine foot named what was already her/his heel   *calcaneous*   about the size of your thumb

OVERTURE
for Frank

Setting free a leaf bright as sunset caught
under the windshield wiper my fingers feel
its ruddy warmth console me as I turn it over
and over in the same trance I felt counting
my newborn's toes Fall has come on short
notice cyans and carotenes doing their usual
work loading up on sugar filtering blue-greens
shining up reds dropping color swatches down

In July when you felled the wasting cherry tree
taking each embracing bough away   you set
a pair of young Zelkova elms in place slender
leafy stanchions soaring skyward beyond my
reach   shedding their splendor now one
touches me   as if to break the coming ice

OHIO APPROACH

Near Cincinnati Kentucky I-75 curves wide before dropping low onto four lane bridge over currents crossed by enslaved persons escaping north An ensouled creature a bridge occasion of awe arcing land to land what was to what will be worth a thought in traffic din mind riveted on next exit ramp consider human worst and best here on my old age pilgrimage road

SOS

Last year's strings   light   full of rain
        of solar   bulbs

and snowmelt   in the yews   lamps still soak
        dangle   three

  noontime   flash   codes all night crimson
up   sun   urgent   to

                    witchhazel

              over
                  and
                      out

SCAVENGER HUNT

One idea of heaven is a place where all lost
things are found   either on display or waiting
close by hidden in the shadows   perpetual light
so annoying I think   and as you search you know
you're getting warm   close enough to hear

    the wedding ring

    daughter's crayoned bittersweet

    old silver tea service

    watercolor of Spinoza's mouse and damselfly
    in their oval pewter frame

    husband's keys to the Subaru

Hear them speaking softly

      Ah   now you're remembering
      where I've been all these years

      Hold me

ABOUT THE AUTHOR

Accents published my first book of poems, *Fountains for Orpheus*, three years ago. Now, at 81 I see *Available Light* as a premature—I hope!—valediction. Mixing memoir, commonplace miracles and recollections, landscapes, loves, and sorrows gleaned from a long and mostly lucky life, these new poems embrace beginnings as well as endings.

    Indebted to countless writers, I find myself turning to the prose and poems of Christian Wiman, Eamon Grennan, and Richard Taylor for their crucial resonance. Among poets no longer living I rely especially on Seamus Heaney and Czeslaw Milosz.

ACKNOWLEDGMENTS

For continued encouragement, I thank the staff at the Carnegie Center for Literacy and Learning, especially Neil Chethik, Marcia Jones, and Jennifer Mattox. Sarah Chapman and Angelica Miller made sure my manuscript files landed properly formatted in Katerina Stoykova's inbox.

Workhorse founder Christopher McCurry's 2017 Poetry Gauntlet challenged nine colleagues, teenaged to octogenarian, to break boundaries along with bagels and donuts. Several *Available Light* poems began life during the Gauntlet.

Kentucky Poet Laureate Jeff Worley's lively Wednesday evening Carnegie class cultivated empathy, keen listening, offered a memorable prompt: a heap of tangled coat hangers.

Worley and Worley! Art historian Michael Worley teamed with brother Jeff for Carnegie's "Writing Poems About Art." Michael's images and Jeff's word crafting illuminated pitfalls in attempting the ekphrastic poem.

Transylvania professor Simonetta Cochis, French and Spanish, and close neighbor Nancy Wolsk, professor emerita, Art History, whose critiquing soirées provided fresh eyes and much merriment.

George Basalla, University of Delaware professor emeritus of history, whose "History of Things" course required weekly essays on the evolution, metaphysics, and poetry of clocks, barbed wire, Coca-Cola cans.

Stanley Brunn, University of Kentucky professor emeritus of geography, for leading me to Yi-Fu Tuan's *Romantic Geography*. No citizen of Earth should be without it.

Frank Hollingshead, creator and keeper of my garden's drift of wild and tame.

Friend from long ago Lee White, who brought me redwing remains one morning, subject of the cover painting.

Contralto and teacher Phyllis Jenness, whose long friendship in song continues to affirm Walter Pater's assertion that "all art aspires toward the condition of music."

Accents Publishing's Dan Klemer, for technical and design savvy, photographing the redwings, proofing, assembling pages, bringing this book to light.

Once again, my thanks to mentor/editor Katerina Stoykova for her vibrant voice and priceless guidance despite iffy Skyping across seven time zones; eye and ear attuned to the line between too much and too little; her gift of the Hopi Three-Step Morning Prayer.

www.ingramcontent.com/pod-product-compliance
Lightning Source LLC
Chambersburg PA
CBHW030140100526
44592CB00011B/973